KENYA TRAVEL GUIDE

2024

YOUR ULTIMATE TRAVEL COMPANION TO EXPLORING A JOURNEY THROUGH WILDLIFE, CULTURE, AND ADVENTURE

Danney P. Porter

WELCOME TO KENYA

Welcome to Kenya, a country renowned for its breathtaking scenery, rich cultural diversity, and wild interior. This travel book is your ticket to an experience through a nation that offers you a distinctive fusion of culture, nature, and adventure. It is a tour that captures the spirit of Africa. We encourage you to explore Kenya's stunning landscapes, rich customs, and exhilarating experiences as you get ready to set out on this once-in-a-lifetime journey.

Why Visit Kenya in 2024?

Kenya is a nation that never stops changing, offering visitors fresh and fascinating experiences each year. The following reasons make 2024 the ideal year to visit Kenya:

The Great Migration: Every year, millions of wildebeest and zebras cross the Maasai Mara in one of nature's most breathtaking spectacles. This animal extravaganza is expected to be even more amazing in 2024.

Cultural Festivals: To honor its many ethnic communities, Kenya organizes several cultural festivals. You can fully immerse yourself in these colorful celebrations in 2024 to learn more about the rich heritage of the nation.

Infrastructure Improvements: Kenya's dedication to tourism has resulted in notable advancements in services, lodging, and transportation, making traveler experiences more pleasurable and comfortable.

Conservation Efforts: Kenya is a favored location for eco-conscious tourists because of its ongoing investments in animal conservation. You'll be able to help these initiatives and witness their results directly.

Community-Based Tourism: Travelers now have more chances than ever to interact with local people and support eco-friendly tourism projects.

A Taste of Adventure: In 2024, Kenya offers exhilarating events ranging from hot air ballooning over the savannah to white-water rafting down the Tana River, catering to both adrenaline junkies and those merely looking for new experiences.

How to Use This Guide

To guarantee that your trip across Kenya is as seamless and rewarding as possible, it's critical to know how to make the most of this guide:

Navigation: The guide is divided into chapters, each of which focuses on a different facet of your trip to Kenya. Using the index at the end of the handbook or using the table of contents will make finding information simple.

Key Information: "Planning Your Trip" contains crucial information about things like currency rates, health advice, and visa requirements.

Destinations: Discover Kenya's many locations, including Mombasa, the idyllic beach town, Maasai Mara, and the busy metropolis of Nairobi. Every place has a specific chapter that provides information on things to see, do, and experience there.

Cultural insights: Explore the chapters devoted to the various ethnic groups and their customs to obtain a greater understanding of Kenya's diverse cultural tapestry.

Adventure & Activities: If you're looking for exhilarating events and activities to get your heart pumping, you will find it here.

Practical Advice: for information on lodging, food options, safety precautions, and environmentally friendly travel.

Sustainability: for information on reducing your environmental effects and helping with conservation efforts.

Resources: helpful websites, emergency numbers, tour operators, and a checklist for travelers.

You'll find a wealth of knowledge and ideas to help you get the most out of your trip to Kenya as you turn the pages of this guide. We hope that this book will be your go-to travel companion, giving you all the resources, you need to make lifelong memories, whether you're an adventurous traveler or a culture vulture. Now let's get the trip started, Karibu Kenya!

KENYA AT A GLANCE

Kenya, often referred to as the "Cradle of Humanity," is a land of breathtaking landscapes, rich cultural diversity, and abundant wildlife. In this chapter, we'll provide an overview of Kenya, touching upon its geography and climate, history and culture, language and communication, and currency and money matters.

Geography and Climate

Geography: Situated in East Africa, Kenya is a country of remarkable geographic diversity. It borders the Indian Ocean to the southeast and is surrounded by Tanzania to the south, Uganda to the west, South Sudan to the northwest, Ethiopia to the north, and Somalia to the northeast.

Kenya's landscape includes coastal plains, highland areas, the Great Rift Valley, and savannahs, providing a range of ecosystems and environments for diverse wildlife.

Climate: Kenya's climate varies depending on the region. The coastal areas have a tropical climate with high humidity and temperatures ranging from 24°C to 30°C (75°F to 86°F). The interior highlands experience a more temperate climate with average temperatures around 10°C to 26°C (50°F to 79°F). The arid and semi-arid regions of northern Kenya have a hot and dry climate with temperatures often exceeding 40°C (104°F). The Great Rift Valley and western Kenya have a moderate climate with temperatures averaging between 11°C to 28°C (52°F to 82°F).

Kenya's climate is influenced by the Indian Ocean, the East African Rift Valley, and the altitude of different regions, resulting in a wide range of temperature and precipitation patterns.

History and Culture

History: Kenya's history is rich and complex. Archaeological evidence suggests that the region has been inhabited for millions of years, and it is often considered the cradle of humanity.

Kenyan history includes the Bantu migrations, the Swahili coast, the arrival of Arab traders, and European colonialism. It gained independence from British colonial rule in 1963 and has since seen significant political, social, and economic developments.

Culture: Kenya is a melting pot of cultures, with over 40 ethnic groups, each contributing to the country's diverse cultural tapestry. The Maasai, Kikuyu, Luo, Luhya, and Swahili cultures are some of the most prominent. Kenya's cultural heritage is expressed through traditional music, dance, art, storytelling, and cuisine.

The country's traditional attire, beadwork, and wood carvings are famous for their artistic value. Kenyans are known for their warm hospitality and strong sense of community.

Language and Communication

Languages: Kenya is a multilingual country with English and Swahili being its official languages. English is widely used for official and educational purposes, while Swahili is the lingua franca, spoken by people from different ethnic backgrounds.

Kenyan Sign Language (KSL) is also recognized as an official language for the deaf community. Additionally, Kenya's ethnic diversity results in numerous indigenous languages, including Kikuyu, Luo, Luhya, and Maasai.

Communication: Kenyans are known for their friendly and open communication style. Handshakes are a common form of greeting. When conversing, it is essential to be polite and respectful. English is widely spoken, making it relatively easy for travelers to communicate. Learning a few basic Swahili phrases can go a long way in building rapport with the locals. Mobile phones are widely used for communication, and Kenya has a well-developed telecommunications infrastructure.

Currency and Money Matters

Currency: The official currency of Kenya is the Kenyan Shilling (KES), often denoted as "Ksh" or simply "Sh." Banknotes and coins of various denominations are in circulation, with the most common banknotes being 50, 100, 200, 500, and 1000 shillings.

Money Matters: Credit and debit cards are widely accepted in urban areas, but cash is still the primary form of payment in more rural regions.

ATMs are easily found in cities and major towns, providing access to cash. It's advisable to carry some cash for purchases in remote areas. When exchanging money, use authorized foreign exchange bureaus or banks for the best rates. Tipping is customary in restaurants and for services like guided tours, and it's appreciated by service providers.

Kenya's geography and climate offer diverse natural landscapes, from the Indian Ocean's sandy shores to the towering peaks of Mount Kenya.

The country's history and culture are deeply rooted in its rich heritage, and its people are known for their warm and welcoming nature. With a multilingual population and a variety of languages spoken, communication in Kenya is generally straightforward, especially when using English or Swahili. Finally, understanding the currency and money practices in Kenya ensures a seamless financial experience during your journey through this captivating country.

PLANNING YOUR TRIP

A successful journey to Kenya begins with thorough planning. This chapter covers essential aspects of preparing for your trip, including visa and entry requirements, vaccinations and health tips, the importance of travel insurance, the best time to visit Kenya, packing essentials, and budgeting for your adventure.

Visa and Entry Requirements

Visa Requirements: Most visitors to Kenya need a visa for entry. Visa requirements vary depending on your nationality, the purpose of your visit, and the length of your stay.

You can check the specific requirements and apply for a visa through the Kenyan government's eVisa portal or consult your nearest Kenyan embassy or consulate. It's advisable to begin the visa application process well in advance of your travel date to allow for processing time.

Passport Requirements: Ensure that your passport is valid for at least six months beyond your intended departure date from Kenya. Additionally, have at least two blank pages in your passport for visa stamps.

Visa on Arrival: Some nationalities are eligible for a visa on arrival, but it's recommended to check the current status with Kenyan immigration authorities before your trip.

Vaccinations and Health Tips

Yellow Fever: Travelers coming from countries with a risk of yellow fever transmission are required to show proof of yellow fever vaccination. Check the World Health Organization (WHO) for a list of countries at risk.

Routine Vaccinations: Ensure your routine vaccinations are up to date. This includes vaccinations for measles, mumps, rubella, diphtheria, tetanus, and pertussis.

Malaria Prevention: Kenya is in a malaria-prone region. Consult your healthcare provider for anti-malarial medication recommendations and use insect repellent and bed nets to prevent mosquito bites.

Water and Food Safety: Drink bottled or purified water and be cautious about food hygiene. Avoid consuming uncooked or undercooked food.

Traveler's Diarrhea: It's advisable to carry over-the-counter medications for traveler's diarrhea in your travel medical kit.

Health Insurance: Consider purchasing travel insurance that includes medical coverage for your trip. In the event of illness or injury, this coverage can be invaluable.

Altitude Sickness: If you plan to visit high-altitude areas, such as the Great Rift Valley or Mount Kenya, be aware of the potential for altitude sickness. Ascend gradually and stay hydrated.

Travel Insurance

Travel insurance is an important component of trip planning. It provides financial protection in case of unforeseen circumstances, such as trip cancellations, medical emergencies, lost luggage, or travel delays.

Ensure your insurance policy covers the specific activities you plan to engage in while in Kenya, especially if you're going on safaris, hiking, or adventure sports. It's recommended to carefully read and understand the terms and conditions of your policy to ensure it meets your needs.

When to Visit Kenya

Kenya's climate and wildlife viewing opportunities vary throughout the year, so choosing the best time to visit is essential:

Dry Season (June to October): This is considered the best time for wildlife safaris in Kenya. The weather is dry and pleasant, making it easier to spot animals congregating around water sources. The Great Migration in the Maasai Mara is a highlight during this period.

Short Rains (November to December): While it's considered the low tourist season, this is a good time to visit Kenya for budget-conscious travelers. The landscape is lush and green, and wildlife is still abundant.

Long Rains (March to May): This is the rainy season, and some areas may become inaccessible due to muddy roads. However, the rains offer spectacular birdwatching and a unique perspective of the landscapes.

Shoulder Seasons: The months of January and February, as well as April and May, are considered shoulder seasons. Prices may be lower, and you can enjoy a balance of good weather and fewer crowds.

Packing Essentials

Clothing: Pack lightweight and breathable clothing suitable for warm temperatures. Layering is a good idea, as it can get cooler in the evenings and at higher altitudes. For safaris, neutral-colored clothing is recommended to avoid disturbing wildlife. Don't forget swimwear for coastal areas.

Footwear: Comfortable walking shoes or hiking boots are essential for exploring national parks and reserves. Sandals or flip-flops are suitable for beach destinations.

Protection from the Elements: Sunscreen, sunglasses, a wide-brimmed hat, and a rain jacket are essential. The African sun can be strong, and sudden rain showers are common.

Safari Gear: If you plan to go on a safari, consider binoculars, a camera with zoom capabilities, and a flashlight for night drives. A small daypack can be useful for carrying essentials during game drives.

Medications: If you have prescription medications, ensure you have an ample supply for your trip. Include a basic first-aid kit with essentials like band-aids, pain relievers, and any necessary personal medications.

Travel Adapters: Kenya uses Type G electrical outlets, so bring the appropriate adapter if your devices have different plug types.

Travel Documents: Keep your passport, visa, and travel insurance documents in a secure and waterproof pouch.

Budgeting for Your Trip

Accommodation: Kenya offers a wide range of accommodation options, from budget hostels and campsites to luxury lodges and hotels. Prices can vary greatly, so research and book accommodations that fit your budget and preferences.

Meals: Eating at local restaurants is often more budget-friendly than dining in hotels. Street food is a popular and affordable option for quick meals. Allow for some splurges on local delicacies and dining experiences.

Safaris and Tours: The cost of safaris and guided tours can vary depending on the duration, activities, and level of luxury. Safaris in private conservancies or exclusive game reserves tend to be more expensive.

Transportation: Domestic flights are convenient for covering long distances. Buses and matatus (shared minivans) are more budget-friendly options. Be prepared for occasional haggling with matatu drivers over fares.

Entrance Fees: National parks and reserves have entrance fees. These fees can vary, so budget accordingly. Some parks offer discounts for residents and East African Community (EAC) citizens.

Extras: Allow for miscellaneous expenses like souvenirs, additional activities, and unforeseen costs.

A well-planned trip to Kenya sets the stage for a memorable and enriching experience. By ensuring you meet visa requirements, taking necessary health precautions, securing travel insurance, choosing the right time to visit, packing wisely, and budgeting appropriately, you can embark on your Kenyan adventure with confidence and peace of mind. Your journey awaits!

NAIROBI - THE CAPITAL CITY

Kenya's dynamic metropolis, Nairobi, offers an enthralling introduction to the nation's unique fusion of urban development, wildlife preservation, and cultural diversity. Nairobi, a city tucked away in the East African savannah, is a place where acacia trees and skyscrapers coexist and where the sounds of everyday life blend with the beckoning of the wild. We will examine Nairobi's most fascinating attractions in this chapter, including its historical sites, distinctive wildlife encounters, and vibrant dining and nightlife scenes.

Exploring Nairobi

The Ambiance of Nairobi: Nairobi has a distinct atmosphere that mixes nature and modernism. While surrounded by the splendor of its natural surroundings, visitors will feel the activity of a city that is expanding quickly. This harmony is perfectly exemplified by the view of skyscrapers set against the backdrop of Nairobi National Park, a wildlife refuge inside the city.

The City Plan: Nairobi is not too difficult to navigate. The city is separated into several distinct neighborhoods, each with its personality. While quiet residential neighborhoods and easy access to the city's top attractions may be found in the suburbs like Karen and Lang'ata, the Central Business District (CBD) serves as the center of government and commerce.

Transportation: Nairobi has a vast network of taxis, matatus (minibuses), and ridesharing services that make getting around the city easier. Additionally, trustworthy automobile rental services are offered by both domestic and foreign companies to visitors. A word of caution: It's vital to schedule your travels appropriately because Nairobi's traffic can be notoriously heavy.

Nairobi National Park

A Wildlife Oasis: Nairobi National Park, known as "The World's Only Wildlife Capital," is evidence of Kenya's dedication to preserving its natural resources. Numerous animals, including lions, giraffes, zebras, and rhinos, may be found at the park, which is only a short drive from the city center.

Safari Walks and Game Drives: Exciting game drives can be had by visitors to Nairobi National Park, either independently or with a tour guide. Another fascinating alternative for people who want to learn more about the ecosystems of the park and get up close and personal with its residents is to take a safari walk.

David Sheldrick Wildlife Trust

Orphaned Elephants: The Nairobi National Park is home to the David Sheldrick Wildlife Trust, which is devoted to the rescue and rehabilitation of elephant and rhino orphans. In addition to viewing these amazing animals, visitors may help with their care by taking part in the "fostering" program.

Education and Conservation: In addition to its primary goal, the trust is vital in spreading awareness of ivory trafficking and the value of preserving these gentle giants. It's a heartfelt educational experience that helps guests grasp wildlife protection on a deeper level.

The Karen Blixen Museum

Out of Africa: Situated in the suburb of Karen, the historical gem is known as the Karen Blixen Museum. Explore her beautifully maintained home and discover more about the life of Danish author Karen Blixen, who gained fame for her memoir "Out of Africa."

African Farmhouse: The museum transports visitors to the colonial era through its attractive African farmhouse setting and displays, pictures, and personal artifacts. For lovers of literature and history, this is a must-visit; the adjacent gardens are as wonderful.

Bomas of Kenya

Exhibition of Cultures: An immersive look into the rich cultural fabric of Kenya's numerous ethnic groups can be had at Bomas of Kenya. It is a living museum that showcases the customs and legacy of several tribes through traditional music, dance, and craft displays for tourists to watch.

Varieties in Performance: The colorful cultural acts are the main attraction when visiting Bomas. Prepare to be enthralled by the captivating dances that retell the myths and tales of Kenya's villages, as well as the rhythmic sounds of traditional instruments.

Nightlife and Dining

Nairobi's Nightlife: Nairobi becomes a metropolis that never sleeps when the sun sets. The city's nighttime sector provides a variety of experiences, ranging from exciting pubs and clubs to live music acts and cultural events.

Districts with a lot of nightlife include the CBD and Westlands.

Dining Delights: Discovering Nairobi's gourmet landscape is an exciting culinary journey. You can enjoy a broad variety of foods, including both international and regional Kenyan fare. A popular dish in Kenya is grilled meat, or if you'd prefer something fancier, check out one of the city's fine dining restaurants.

Kenya's vibrant capital, Nairobi, is a city full of surprises and contrasts. Nairobi has enough to offer every type of visitor, from its abundant wildlife inside the city boundaries to its rich cultural history and exciting nightlife.

Regardless of your interests—nature, history, or cuisine— Nairobi provides an experience that will never be forgotten, leaving you enthralled and wanting to see more of Kenya. So take a deep breath of Nairobi's vitality and start exploring this amazing city!

WILDLIFE SAFARI

Going on a wildlife safari in Kenya is like taking a trip right into the center of one of the most breathtaking natural theaters on the planet. The vast assortment of animals found in the nation's many landscapes and ecosystems provides a front-row seat to some of Mother Nature's most spectacular displays.

This chapter will walk you through the best places in Kenya to go on safari, from the well-known Maasai Mara National Reserve to the undiscovered gems of Samburu National Reserve. We'll also give you important safari etiquette and guidelines so that your safari is a courteous and safe experience.

The Great Migration

A Natural Marvel: One of the world's most amazing wildlife shows is the Great Migration. See the migratory patterns of millions of wildebeest, zebras, and other herbivores as they cross the Maasai Mara in Kenya and the Serengeti in Tanzania in search of better pastures.

Timing Your Visit: It's important to schedule your visit for the appropriate time of year if you want to witness this spectacular event. Although the precise time can vary, the migration usually takes place between July and September. To make sure you're in the right area at the right time, do your homework and speak with local guides.

Game Drives and Balloon Safaris: The most well-liked method of seeing the Great Migration is during game drives. A lot of resorts and tour companies provide guided drives to some of the best viewpoints. A hot air balloon safari over the enormous herds is an amazing experience that offers a unique viewpoint and stunning vistas.

Maasai Mara National Reserve

Iconic Safari Destination: An African trip is not complete without a visit to the Maasai Mara. It's a wildlife enthusiast's dream come true because of its breathtaking environment, varied fauna, and predator-prey interactions.

Big Five Encounters: You will come across the Big Five (lion, elephant, buffalo, leopard, and rhinoceros) as well as several other species on the grassy plains and acacia-dotted landscapes of the Mara. There is a good chance that visitors to Maasai Mara game drives will see these magnificent creatures in their native environment.

Maasai Culture: The Maasai people live in the Mara region and are distinguished by their bright red dress and beaded jewelry. Cultural safari the safari is getting to know the Maasai people and their way of life.

Amboseli National Park

Majestic Kilimanjaro Views: Africa's highest mountain, Mount Kilimanjaro, is visible from Amboseli. A beautiful scene is created by the snow-capped peak against the savannah.

Elephants and Birdlife: The park is well-known for its abundant birdlife and sizable herds of elephants. Elephant herds are frequently spotted against Kilimanjaro's breathtaking backdrop, making it a popular destination for wildlife photography.

Tsavo National Parks

Vast Wilderness: Tsavo East and Tsavo West, the two parks that makeup Tsavo National Park, are renowned for their vast expanses and untamed environments. Because it's a less busy safari location, you can get closer to the animals.

Varied Wildlife: Both parks are home to a variety of bird species and a vast array of wildlife, including the Big Five. Tsavo is renowned for its "red elephants," which seem to be marred by the red dust of the park.

Lake Nakuru National Park

Birdwatcher's Paradise: Flamingo populations in Lake Nakuru are well-known for their ability to transform the lake's surface into an enchanting shade of pink. It is an important nesting area for these birds.

Rhinoceros Conservation: There are continuous efforts to save the black and white rhinoceros populations that find refuge in the park.

Samburu National Reserve

Hidden Gem: Reticulated giraffes, Grevy's zebras, Somali ostriches, gerenuks, and Beisa oryxes are among the rare species found in the less-traveled Samburu National Reserve.

Cultural Encounters: This area is home to a separate ethnic group known as the Samburu people. Experiencing their villages and discovering their way of life adds an intriguing cultural element to your safari.

Safari Tips and Etiquette

Responsible Safari Practices:

Respect for Wildlife: Keep a safe distance from all animals and refrain from stressing them out or interfering with their activity.

Leave No Trace: Adhere to the guidelines of responsible tourism and make sure you don't leave any trash or litter behind

Encourage Conservation: To help preserve Kenya's priceless ecosystems, think about making a donation or offering your time to wildlife conservation groups.

Safety Measures: Listen to Your Guides: Since your safari guides are knowledgeable about the area, pay great attention to what they say and do what they advise.

Vehicle Safety: When going on game drives, stay inside the car and follow all safety instructions to protect yourself.

Cultural Sensitivity

Respect Local Customs: Be mindful of the customs of the people you are engaging with and get their permission before snapping pictures.

Dress Code: Show respect for local customs by wearing modest apparel when visiting rural areas and communities.

Environmental Awareness

Minimize Plastic Use: By using reusable water bottles and cutting down on plastic trash, you may lessen your impact on the environment.

Off-Roading: Avoid damaging sensitive ecosystems by only going off-road when essential and under a guide's supervision.

Your wildlife safari in Kenya is sure to be an amazing experience. These best safari locations provide a wide variety of experiences, ranging from the calm of Amboseli and the cultural diversity of Samburu to the majesty of the Maasai Mara.

Through observance of ethical safari behaviors and consideration of the guidance provided in this chapter, you may guarantee a tour through Kenya's breathtaking natural environment that is safe, courteous, and truly inspiring. So grab your binoculars and camera, and get ready for an adventure that will allow you to experience Africa's untamed side.

COASTAL PARADISE - MOMBASA AND DIANI

Kenya's Indian Ocean coast is a tropical paradise renowned for its immaculate beaches, lively culture, and thrilling water sports.

We'll take you through the coastal jewels of Mombasa and Diani in this chapter, sharing information on the historical landmarks in Mombasa City, the breathtaking Diani Beach, and the fascinating fusion of Swahili food and culture.

Mombasa City

Gateway to the Coast: The second-biggest city in Kenya, Mombasa, is the entry point to the coastal area. With a distinctive fusion of Indian, Arabian, and African elements, it is a thriving metropolis with a unique coastal culture.

Old Town and Fort Jesus: The Old Town of Mombasa, which is home to lively markets, narrow, winding lanes, and Swahili architecture, is recognized as a UNESCO World Heritage Site. Fort Jesus, an impressive 16th-century Portuguese castle that provides a window into Mombasa's rich past, is the jewel in the crown of Old Town.

Fort Jesus Museum: The museum, which is housed inside Fort Jesus, has a collection of relics that provide visitors with a clearer understanding of the city's past. These artifacts include weapons, earthenware, and pottery. Take in the breathtaking view of the Indian Ocean from the fort's walls.

Historic Mombasa

Swahili Culture and Architecture: An immense collection of Swahili culture and architecture may be found in Old Town Mombasa. Traditional Swahili designs, elaborate balconies, and unique carved wooden doors are the result of the blending of Arab, Indian, and African influences.

Spice Markets and Bazaars: Discover the vibrant bazaars and fragrant spice markets of Old Town. An enormous variety of spices, fabrics, jewelry, and traditional crafts are abundant in these markets. Having conversations with neighborhood business owners offers an opportunity to experience real Swahili culture.

Diani Beach

Paradise on the South Coast: About an hour's drive from Mombasa, Diani Beach is a pristine coastal paradise known for its pristine white sand and glistening waves. It is regularly ranked as one of the best beaches in the world.

Water Adventures: Diani Beach provides a variety of aquatic experiences. Aquatic thrills abound, with activities like deep-sea fishing, windsurfing, kite surfing, and snorkeling on colorful coral reefs.

The Colobus Conservation: The Colobus Conservation, an important project aimed at preserving the Angolan colobus monkey, is also based in Diani. Not only can visitors see these amazing animals in the wild, but they can also learn about conservation efforts.

Snorkeling and Water Sports

Diving into the Coral Gardens: There are excellent snorkeling and diving options at Mombasa and Diani. Under the Indian Ocean, there is a kaleidoscope of marine life visible in the coral gardens, including vibrant fish, rays, and even turtles. Take advantage of experienced diving instructors to discover the underwater world, or sign up for all-level snorkeling tours.

Water Sports Extravaganza: Along the coast, paddleboarding, kite surfing, and windsurfing are all very popular water sports. The steady trade winds make the ideal setting for these thrilling pursuits. Rentals of both equipment and lessons are easily accessible.

Deep-Sea Fishing: Deep-sea fishing is a heavenly experience in the waters off the coast of Kenya. Skilled fishermen can try their hand at capturing tuna, sailfish, marlin, and other species. Everyone may enjoy this accessible adventure thanks to fishing guides and charter boats.

Swahili Cuisine

Flavorful Delights: The Swahili people's food is a beautiful blend of Indian, Arabian, and African flavors. Savor the mouthwatering flavors of Swahili cuisine, which mostly consists of coconut, rice, fresh seafood, and flavorful spices. Biryani, pilau, and the famous Swahili coconut fish stew are must-tries.

Street Food Adventures: Explore the streets of Diani and Mombasa to find a plethora of street food vendors. Savor regional specialties such as cassava chips, mahamri (deep-fried dough), and samosas. In addition to tantalizing your taste senses, street food provides a genuine window into the way of life in the area.

Dining by the Sea: Savor seafood delicacies in eateries with views of the water. Eating by the sea is an incredibly unique experience since freshly caught fish and shellfish are served to absolute perfection. Enjoy your meal with a taste of spiced Swahili tea or tropical fruit juices.

The coastal gems of Kenya, Mombasa, and Diani, offer an enticing fusion of culture, nature, and history. Visitors may enjoy the best of coastal Kenya, from the historical treasures of Mombasa City to the picturesque beaches of Diani.

Take in the breathtaking undersea scenery, embrace the many cultural influences, and indulge in the mouthwatering tastes of Swahili cuisine. You should come away from this trip with enduring recollections of Kenya's gorgeous coastal region. It promises to be both energizing and enriching.

THE RIFT VALLEY

A geological wonder, Kenya's Great Rift Valley captivates visitors looking for a unique combination of vibrant wildlife, spectacular landscapes, and geological structures.

This chapter will cover a variety of topics, including the breathtaking Rift Valley, the calm waters of Lake Naivasha, a visit to the flamingo-filled Lake Bogoria, relaxing by the lakeshore of Lake Baringo, and the untamed Elmenteita Badlands.

Great Rift Valley

Geological Marvel: Kenya is lucky to have a sizable piece of the 6,000-kilometer Great Rift Valley, a geological trench that runs from the Middle East to Mozambique. Throughout millions of years, the valley's formation has produced a variety of landscapes, from lush farmlands to steep escarpments.

Rift Valley Lakes: Numerous freshwater and saltwater lakes, each distinctive in its own right, are spaced throughout the Great Rift Valley. From high spots along the escarpment, visitors can take in breath-taking vistas of these lakes.

Lake Naivasha

Picturesque Water: Freshwater Lake Naivasha is well known for its peace and picturesque surroundings. It's a haven for birdwatchers and wildlife lovers, surrounded by volcanic craters and acacia trees.

Birdwatching Paradise: The lake is a birdwatcher's paradise because of its diverse birdlife. Many species, such as kingfishers, pelicans, and fish eagles, may be visible to you.

Boat Safaris: Boat safaris at Lake Naivasha provide guests the chance to get up close and personal with hippos and a variety of waterfowl. These leisurely outings offer a tranquil approach to take in the natural beauty of the lake.

Hell's Gate National Park

Geological Spectacles: A geological marvel, Hell's Gate National Park features breathtaking gorges, geothermal springs, and towering red cliffs. The theme park was the source of inspiration for Disney's "The Lion King."

Hiking and Biking Adventures: A great place to go hiking and mountain biking is Hell's Gate. The extensive path system enables visitors to explore the park's remarkable scenery and leads to some of the best overlooks.

Geothermal Activity: Hot springs and geysers that erupt from the ground are examples of the geothermal activity that occurs in the park. The first geothermal power plant in Africa is located in Hell's Gate, and guests may learn more about this renewable energy source by going on guided tours of the facility.

Lake Bogoria

Flamingo Spectacle: Flamingos that live at Lake Bogoria are well known for congregating around the coastline for food. It's an amazing sight to see thousands of pink flamingos against the turquoise waters of the lake.

Geysers and Hot Springs: The shoreline of the lake is peppered with hot springs and geysers, resulting in a singular fusion of geothermal activity and scenic beauty. Discovering these things allows visitors to take in the breathtaking scenery.

Lake Baringo

Tranquil Oasis: Lake Baringo is a lesser-known jewel in the Rift Valley, a tranquil refuge. The verdant surroundings of the lake offer the perfect setting for unwinding and birding.

Birding Delights: Baringo is a birdwatcher's dream come true, with records of over 470 species. The fish eagle, the Goliath heron, and several kingfishers are among the highlights. The best approach to interacting with the local birds is through boat safaris.

The Elmenteita Badlands

Rugged Terrain: Situated near Lake Elmenteita, the Elmenteita Badlands are a distinctive terrain consisting of worn volcanic rock formations. There are exploration and photo possibilities in the bizarre surroundings.

Lesser-Known Treasure: Because there aren't as many tourists in this area, it's the perfect getaway for anyone looking for seclusion and adventure.

The lush, varied landscapes that geological forces have sculpted are a tribute to their strength and beauty, as demonstrated by the Rift Valley. This chapter has given you an overview of the distinctive sights that the Rift Valley has to offer, from the placid shores of Lake Baringo to the flaming spectacle of Hell's Gate, the pink-hued splendor of Lake Bogoria, and the tranquility of Lake Naivasha. A lifetime of memories awaits you in the Rift Valley, whether you are an adventure seeker, animal fanatic, or just a tourist looking for off-the-beaten-path experiences.

MOUNT KENYA AND THE HIGHLANDS

The breathtakingly beautiful central highlands of Kenya, which include the majestic Mount Kenya, are a haven for those who love the outdoors and adventure.

We'll travel through Mount Kenya National Park, learn about the hiking and trekking paths that ascend to its summits, discover the varied scenery of Aberdare National Park, pay a visit to the verdant tea plantations, and fully engage in the rich cultural experiences of the highlands in this chapter.

Mount Kenya National Park

Africa's Second-Highest Peak: The second-highest peak in Africa and the highest peak in Kenya, Mount Kenya, provides hikers and mountaineers with amazing views. A UNESCO World Heritage Site, its craggy summits are covered in glaciers.

Hiking and Climbing: For hikers of all skill levels, the park offers a network of well-maintained paths. A thrilling experience for those looking for a more difficult adventure is climbing Mount Kenya's peaks, which include Point Lenana, Batian, and Nelion.

Unique Animals and Plants: The slopes of Mount Kenya are home to an astounding variety of ecosystems, ranging from alpine desert to montane forest. A variety of plants and animals, including rare and endemic species, can be found here. Look out for the vibrant, otherworldly lobelias and the endearing black-and-white colobus monkey.

Hiking and Trekking Routes

Sirimon Route: For hikers, one of the most well-liked and easily accessible trails is the Sirimon Route. It offers the chance to go through several ecological zones, such as the alpine desert, moorlands, and lush rainforest.

Chogoria Route: The breathtaking vistas along this road make it a favorite. Hikers can enjoy stunning views of the summits as they travel through pristine glacier valleys on the Chogoria Route.

Naro Moru Route: Point Lenana can be reached more quickly and directly via the Naro Moru Route. For hikers who are pressed for time or who want a more strenuous ascent, it's an excellent choice.

Burguret Route: The Burguret Route is a less-trod path for the daring and experienced hiker. It offers seclusion and an untainted, rocky nature experience.

Aberdare National Park

The Queen's Bastion: Known as the "Queen's Bastion," Aberdare National Park is a verdant, hilly haven with a wide variety of species. It's one of Kenya's most accessible highland parks and home to the Big Five.

The Ark Lodge: The Ark Lodge is a distinctive tree lodge in Aberdare that offers visitors the amazing chance to see wildlife right from their rooms. It is especially well-known for the floodlit waterhole that draws animals all night long.

Game Drives and Birdwatching: Game drives, narrated nature walks, and superb birdwatching possibilities are available to visitors. Aberdare is a wildlife enthusiast's dream because it is home to numerous rare and endangered species.

Tea Plantations

Lush Green Landscapes: Tea farms stretch for miles in the highlands, creating a patchwork of verdant surroundings. This area is known for its important tea business, and seeing rows of perfectly manicured tea plants is a sight to behold.

Limuru and Kericho: Major tea-producing regions are Limuru, which is close to Nairobi, and Kericho, which is further west. In addition to sampling freshly brewed Kenyan tea, visitors may watch the tea-making process in action by joining guided tours of tea factories.

Cultural Experiences

Engaging with Local Communities: Discovering the highlands is much more than simply the natural beauty. Additionally, guests can interact with the nearby Embu and Kikuyu people. You will have the opportunity to learn about customs, everyday life, and folklore.

Traditional Cuisine: Sample regional cuisine cooked by traditional Kenyan cooks. Taste ugali (maize porridge), nyama choma (grilled meat), and other stews, all imbued with real flavors and provided with a friendly greeting.

Kenya is incredibly diverse, as evidenced by the highlands of Mount Kenya and Aberdare National Park, which provide a unique combination of adventure, natural beauty, and cultural immersion.

The highlands offer an enlightening and engrossing journey for all types of travelers: experienced hikers ascending the peaks of Mount Kenya, wildlife enthusiasts discovering Aberdare's varied ecosystems, tea connoisseurs sipping freshly brewed tea in the plantations, and tourists looking for real cultural experiences. As varied and amazing as the surroundings themselves are going to be the memories you make here.

CULTURAL ENCOUNTERS

Kenya's dynamic and diverse groups, each with its traditions, dialects, and customs, are reflected in the country's rich cultural tapestry.

We'll travel across several cultures in this chapter, encountering the well-known Maasai and Samburu tribes, taking in the coastal Swahili culture, learning about the customs of the Kikuyu, Luo, and Luhya people, and discovering the fascinating world of traditional dance, music, art, and crafts.

The Maasai People

The Iconic Maasai: Among Kenya's ethnic groups, the Maasai are arguably the most well-known due to their unusual attire, beaded crafts, and traditional customs. They live in southern Kenya and the Great Rift Valley.

Colorful Attire: A visual feast of vivid reds, blues, and purples may be seen in Maasai dress. They dress in headdresses, called shōkàs (sheets of fabric), and ornate jewelry. Each design and color has a distinct meaning.

Traditional Dances: The Maasai people are renowned for their vibrant dances, which frequently feature leaps from great heights and expressive gestures. Visitors are treated to a thrilling experience as their music and dance are an essential part of their rituals and celebrations.

Livestock and Nomadic Lifestyle: The Maasai are pastoralists who depend on animals, especially cattle. Because of their nomadic lifestyle, they regularly relocate in search of new pastures for their animals.

Samburu Tribes

Rugged Samburu Region: The people known as Samburu are from the untamed north of Kenya. They both live pastoral lifestyles and wear traditional dress, which are aspects of their shared culture with the Maasai.

Beaded Adornments: Beaded ornaments and jewelry are an integral aspect of Samburu culture. Their beading has symbolic patterns and colors, and different pieces communicate different ideas.

Strong Community Ties: Well-known for their close-knit communities are the Samburu people. They celebrate life transitions and celebrations together, and their social structure is based on age groups.

Ceremonial Rituals: An essential component of Samburu culture is ceremonial life. Rituals, music, and dance are used to celebrate rites of passage like marriage and initiation.

Swahili Culture

Coastal Influences: The dynamic blend of African, Arabian, and Indian traditions known as Swahili culture has a strong influence on Kenya's coastal region. The most notable places to find it are Mombasa, Lamu, and Zanzibar.

Unique Architecture: Winding lanes, coral stone structures, and finely carved wooden doors are hallmarks of Swahili architecture. Explore the charm of Mombasa's and Lamu's historic cities.

The Art of Cuisine: The food of the Swahili people is a culinary journey. Indulge your palate with specialties like pilau, biryani, and the well-known Swahili coconut fish stew. These tastes offer a unique culinary experience.

Dhows and Maritime Culture: The sea has a significant role in Swahili culture. Dhow tours are a popular way for tourists to see the coastal waterways. Dhows are historic sailing vessels.

Kikuyu, Luo, and Luhya Cultures

The Kikuyu People: In Kenya, the Kikuyu constitute the largest ethnic group. They are well-known for their colorful Mau Mau history and agricultural customs, and they live in the central highlands.

The Luo Community: The Luo people live mostly near Lake Victoria in western Kenya. Their rich cultural legacy includes the traditional boat dance, benga music, and the recognizable Luo guitar.

The Luhya Tribes: The western region of Kenya is home to the Luhya people. Numerous subgroups have affected their culture, and traditional dances, drumming, and food are features of their festivals.

Traditional Music and Dance

Rhythmic Expressions: A plethora of traditional music and dances showcase Kenya's cultural richness. Every town has its distinctive dances, tunes, and rhythms, which frequently accompanied by vintage instruments like drums, flutes, and stringed instruments.

Ceremonial Celebrations: A lot of events, such as those for initiations, weddings, funerals, and births, are celebrated with music and dance. These shows are important for communicating happiness, grief, and solidarity among communities.

Art and Crafts

Creative Expression: Kenyan artists are well-known for their skills. Discover how traditional goods, including paintings, carvings, and elaborate beadwork, are made by exploring markets and workshops.

Souvenirs and Gifts: Crafts and artwork provide memorable and distinctive keepsakes. You can purchase a variety of artistic artifacts to take home, such as handwoven baskets, carved wooden masks, and Maasai beading.

Cultural exchanges in Kenya provide a window into the richness and diversity of the nation's population. Kenya's cultural diversity is an integral aspect of any trip through this amazing country, whether you're experiencing the well-known customs of the Maasai and Samburu, immersing yourself in Swahili coastal culture, or learning about the heritage of the Kikuyu, Luo, and Luhya communities.

Experiencing traditional music, dance, art, and crafts enhances one's appreciation of Kenya's fascinating past.

ADVENTURE BEYOND SAFARIS

While Kenya is famed for its magnificent wildlife safaris, there's a world of adventure waiting for those who want a thrill beyond the savannas. In this chapter, we'll discover fascinating activities that take you beyond the standard safari experience.

From drifting high above the landscapes in a hot air balloon to the adrenaline-pumping adventures of white-water rafting, rock climbing, and caving, and from peaceful birdwatching to the elegance of horseback riding and the thrill of paragliding, Kenya offers a diverse array of thrilling experiences for adventure enthusiasts.

Hot Air Ballooning

A Serene Aerial Journey: Drifting high above the Maasai Mara or the Great Rift Valley in a hot air balloon provides a unique perspective on Kenya's stunning landscapes. The silence of the skies and the gentle breeze make this an unforgettable experience.

Dawn Safaris: Hot air balloon safaris often take place at dawn, providing a serene yet awe-inspiring experience as you watch the world below come to life. Keep an eye out for wildlife, especially as you approach the Mara River during the Great Migration.

Champagne Breakfast: The adventure concludes with a champagne breakfast in the bush, surrounded by the pristine wilderness, making this a perfect romantic outing or a unique way to celebrate a special occasion.

White-Water Rafting

Thrills on the Rapids: Kenya offers incredible white-water rafting experiences, particularly on the Tana River and the Athi-Galana-Sabaki River. Rapids vary in difficulty, making this an adventure suitable for both beginners and experienced rafters.

Scenic Gorges and Wildlife: As you navigate the exhilarating rapids, you'll pass through scenic gorges and might spot wildlife along the riverbanks, creating a perfect blend of adrenaline and natural beauty.

Rafting Camps: Rafting operators typically offer camping options, allowing you to fully immerse yourself in the adventure. Staying in these camps provides an opportunity to bond with fellow adventurers and share stories around the campfire.

Rock Climbing and Caving

Hell's Gate Climbing: Hell's Gate National Park offers an excellent rock climbing experience, with various routes catering to different skill levels. The stunning cliffs, dramatic landscapes, and the opportunity to explore volcanic formations make this an adventure like no other.

Ngare Ndare Forest Reserve: Ngare Ndare Forest Reserve is home to a unique canopy walkway and beautiful turquoise pools. The area also offers excellent rock climbing opportunities, making it a great day trip from Nanyuki or Meru.

Caving in Mount Elgon: The caves of Mount Elgon, in western Kenya, offer an underground adventure. These subterranean chambers are both mysterious and awe-inspiring, with guided tours providing insights into the geological wonders hidden beneath the earth's surface.

Bird Watching

A Birder's Paradise: Kenya's diverse ecosystems, including forests, wetlands, and savannas, are a haven for birdwatching enthusiasts. The country boasts over 1,000 bird species, including numerous endemics and migratory birds.

Iconic Birding Spots: Birdwatchers can explore prime locations like Lake Nakuru, Lake Naivasha, and Kakamega Forest, each teeming with avian wonders. Don't forget to visit the Maasai Mara and the Great Rift Valley for spectacular sightings.

Guided Tours: Professional birdwatching guides can provide insights into Kenya's birdlife, ensuring you don't miss out on any rare or elusive species. Consider joining birdwatching tours to enhance your experience.

Horseback Riding

Equestrian Adventures: Kenya's diverse landscapes offer an ideal backdrop for horseback riding. From the foothills of Mount Kenya to the Maasai Mara, there are riding safaris catering to riders of all levels.

Unique Safaris: Horseback safaris allow you to access remote areas that are often inaccessible by vehicles. It's a quieter and more immersive way to observe wildlife while savoring the elegance of the equine experience.

Exploring the Great Rift Valley: Riding along the escarpment of the Great Rift Valley offers breathtaking views and a serene connection to nature. The unique perspective from horseback adds an extra layer of wonder to your adventure.

Paragliding

Soaring with the Birds: Paragliding offers the exhilarating experience of soaring above Kenya's scenic landscapes. It's a unique way to admire the beauty of the Rift Valley, Aberdare ranges, and the Great Rift Valley lakes.

Tandem Flights: Tandem paragliding flights are available for those new to the sport, providing a safe and thrilling experience as you glide over Kenya's natural wonders.

Aerial Photography: The freedom and perspective paragliding offers make it a fantastic choice for aerial photographers, enabling them to capture stunning landscapes and wildlife from above.

Adventure in Kenya goes far beyond traditional safaris. Whether you're floating silently above the Maasai Mara in a hot air balloon, navigating white-water rapids, climbing rugged cliffs, exploring underground caves, observing diverse birdlife, riding through pristine landscapes on horseback, or soaring high with the birds through paragliding, Kenya's offerings are as diverse as its landscapes. These adventures provide unique and unforgettable experiences for those who seek excitement and a deeper connection with the natural world.

PRACTICAL INFORMATION

Practical information is vital for a smooth and enjoyable journey through Kenya. In this chapter, we'll provide insights into getting around the country, the range of accommodation options available, dining and cuisine experiences, ensuring your safety during your travels, and practicing sustainable and responsible tourism.

Getting Around Kenya

Modes of Transportation: Kenya offers various means of transportation to get around, depending on your preferences and budget. These include domestic flights, matatus (shared minivans), buses, trains, taxis, and car rentals.

Domestic Flights: Domestic flights are a convenient way to cover long distances quickly. Airports in Nairobi, Mombasa, and Eldoret serve as major domestic flight hubs, connecting you to various destinations across the country.

Matatus and Buses: Matatus are shared minivans that provide a cost-effective means of traveling within cities and between towns. Buses, on the other hand, are typically more spacious and comfortable and are commonly used for longer journeys.

Train Travel: Kenya has been expanding its railway network, making train travel a more viable option. The Madaraka Express runs between Nairobi and Mombasa and offers a comfortable and scenic journey.

Taxis and Ride-Sharing: Taxis are readily available in urban areas, offering a convenient way to get around the city. Ride-sharing apps like Uber are also popular in Nairobi and Mombasa.

Car Rentals: For those seeking more flexibility and autonomy, renting a car is an option. Ensure you have the appropriate permits, and be prepared for varied road conditions, especially in more remote areas.

Accommodation Options

Wide Range of Choices: Kenya offers a diverse array of accommodation options to suit all budgets and preferences. These include luxury lodges, boutique hotels, safari camps, budget hostels, and even camping.

Safari Lodges and Camps: Safari lodges and tented camps provide a unique and immersive experience in the heart of wildlife-rich national parks. These range from luxurious options to more budget-friendly choices.

Boutique Hotels and Resorts: Urban areas like Nairobi and coastal destinations like Mombasa boast a range of boutique hotels and luxury resorts, offering comfort and relaxation.

Hostels and Guesthouses: Budget travelers can find hostels and guesthouses in cities and tourist hubs. These offer affordable accommodations with basic amenities and a chance to meet fellow travelers.

Camping: Camping is a popular choice for those seeking a closer connection with nature. Many national parks offer designated campsites, and there are specialized camping safaris available.

Food and Dining

Diverse Cuisine: Kenyan cuisine is as diverse as the country itself. It includes influences from various communities, such as the Swahili, Maasai, and Indian. Popular dishes include nyama choma (grilled meat), ugali (maize porridge), and a variety of stews.

Street Food Adventures: Exploring street food is a fantastic way to experience local flavors. Try delicious samosas, mahamri (deep-fried dough), cassava crisps, and the ubiquitous chapati.

Dining Out: Kenya's urban areas offer a wide selection of international restaurants, from Italian to Chinese. Nairobi, in particular, has a thriving culinary scene with many upscale dining options.

Hydration: While tap water in Nairobi and other major cities is generally safe to drink, tourists should stick to bottled or filtered water, especially in more remote areas.

Staying Safe

Health Precautions: Before traveling to Kenya, it's essential to check for recommended vaccinations and take malaria prophylactics, especially if you plan to visit high-risk areas. Carry insect repellent and take precautions against mosquito bites.

Wildlife Safety: While observing wildlife is a primary attraction in Kenya, it's crucial to do so safely. Keep a respectful distance from animals and follow the guidance of your guides to ensure your safety and the animal's well-being.

Cultural Sensitivity: Kenya's diverse cultures should be respected. Dress modestly, especially in rural and conservative areas, and ask for permission before taking photos of local people.

Security: Kenya is generally safe for tourists. However, exercise caution in crowded areas, and keep an eye on your belongings. Avoid displaying valuable items and be wary of petty theft.

Travel Insurance: It's advisable to have comprehensive travel insurance, covering medical emergencies, trip cancellations, and personal belongings.

Sustainable Travel Practices

Responsible Wildlife Viewing: Choose tour operators and guides who prioritize responsible wildlife viewing and conservation. Support organizations dedicated to protecting Kenya's natural heritage.

Eco-Friendly Accommodation: Opt for lodges, camps, and hotels that practice sustainable tourism, such as using renewable energy sources, reducing waste, and supporting local communities.

Wildlife Conservation Initiatives: Consider participating in or supporting wildlife conservation programs and sanctuaries, which play a vital role in protecting Kenya's endangered species.

Reduce Plastic Waste: Carry a reusable water bottle and shopping bag to minimize plastic waste. Many areas have banned single-use plastic bags, so be prepared.

Local Communities: Engage with local communities respectfully and ethically. Support local artisans, markets, and craftspeople, ensuring your purchases benefit the local economy.

Traveling in Kenya is a rewarding adventure, whether you're exploring the wildlife-rich national parks, delving into the country's rich cultural tapestry, or seeking thrilling outdoor activities.

By following practical information on transportation, accommodation, dining, safety, and sustainable travel practices, you can ensure a memorable and responsible journey through this diverse and captivating country.

KENYA'S ISLANDS AND LAKES

Kenya's landscape is defined not only by its vast savannas and wildlife-rich national parks but also by a collection of serene islands and stunning lakes.

In this chapter, we'll explore some of Kenya's most captivating islands and lakes, including the tranquil Lamu Island, the dramatic Lake Turkana, the expansive Lake Victoria, and the opportunities for island hopping, fishing, and a variety of water activities that these water bodies offer.

Lamu Island

A Timeless Gem: Lamu Island, a UNESCO World Heritage Site, is a captivating island that has retained its timeless charm. This cultural melting pot is a glimpse into the Swahili way of life.

Architecture and History: The narrow streets of Lamu are lined with coral stone buildings adorned with intricately carved wooden doors. The island's history is intertwined with Arab and Portuguese influences.

Donkeys and No Cars: One of Lamu's distinctive features is the absence of cars. Donkeys are the primary mode of transportation, contributing to the island's serene and peaceful atmosphere.

Waterfront Vibes: Lamu's waterfront is bustling with dhows and traditional fishing boats. Stroll along the seafront, visit the Lamu Museum, and explore the island's rich culture.

Lake Turkana

The Jade Sea: Lake Turkana, often referred to as the "Jade Sea" due to its distinctive blue-green color, is the largest desert lake in the world. Its dramatic landscapes and arid surroundings are a testament to nature's awe-inspiring power.

UNESCO World Heritage Site: Lake Turkana is a UNESCO World Heritage Site, known for its unique geological features and rich paleontological history. It's home to fossil remains of some of the earliest humans and hominids.

Turkana Tribes: The indigenous Turkana people inhabit the surrounding areas. Their nomadic way of life and traditional practices are deeply rooted in the harsh terrain of the Turkana region.

Fishing and Water Activities: Fishing in Lake Turkana is a significant livelihood for local communities. Visitors can engage in fishing activities, go on boat trips, or simply soak in the striking beauty of the lake.

Lake Victoria

The Great Lake: Lake Victoria, Africa's largest lake and the world's second-largest freshwater lake, is a vast expanse of water shared by Kenya, Tanzania, and Uganda. Its shores are dotted with towns and fishing communities.

Breathtaking Sunsets: The sunsets over Lake Victoria are legendary. From various vantage points along the lake, you can witness the sun setting in a blaze of colors over the tranquil waters.

Birdwatching: Lake Victoria is a haven for birdwatchers, with numerous species of birds residing in the wetlands and islands that dot the lake. Rusinga Island and Mfangano Island are notable birdwatching destinations.

Fishing Communities: Fishing is a way of life for many communities along the lake. Engage with local fishermen and explore their daily activities, or try your hand at fishing for Nile perch.

Island Hopping

Discovering Kenya's Archipelagos: Kenya's coast is dotted with beautiful archipelagos, including the Lamu Archipelago, the Pate Islands, and the Kiunga Marine National Reserve. Island hopping allows you to explore the diverse landscapes and cultures of these islands.

Pate Island: Pate Island, part of the Lamu Archipelago, boasts the historical town of Pate, ancient ruins, and pristine beaches. It's a quiet and unspoiled island that offers a serene escape.

Kiunga Marine National Reserve: The Kiunga Marine National Reserve is a protected area that encompasses the Kiwayu archipelago. It's an excellent location for snorkeling, scuba diving, and experiencing marine life.

Fishing and Water Activities

Fishing Expeditions: Kenya's lakes and coastal waters offer exceptional fishing opportunities. Lake Victoria, Lake Turkana, and the Indian Ocean are known for their diverse fish species, including the iconic Nile perch.

Water Sports: Water sports enthusiasts can enjoy activities like windsurfing, kitesurfing, and paddleboarding along the coast. Diani Beach and Watamu are popular destinations for these activities.

Diving and Snorkeling: The Kenyan coast offers some of the best diving and snorkeling sites in East Africa. Explore colorful coral reefs, shipwrecks, and vibrant marine life in destinations like Watamu and Diani.

Kenya's islands and lakes offer a unique perspective on the country's diverse geography and culture. From the timeless charm of Lamu Island to the dramatic landscapes of Lake Turkana and the vast expanse of Lake Victoria, these destinations are rich in natural beauty and cultural experiences.

Whether you're exploring island archipelagos, engaging with fishing communities, or participating in water activities, Kenya's islands and lakes provide a wealth of adventures and memories to cherish.

SOUVENIRS AND SHOPPING

Exploring the markets and shopping districts of Kenya is a delightful way to immerse yourself in the local culture and bring back meaningful souvenirs from your journey. In this chapter, we'll guide you through the best markets and shopping districts, introduce you to popular Kenyan souvenirs, and offer bargaining tips to help you make the most of your shopping experiences.

Best Markets and Shopping Districts

Maasai Market, Nairobi: Located in various locations in Nairobi, the Maasai Market is a vibrant and bustling place where you can find a wide range of Maasai crafts, jewelry, and traditional clothing. It's a must-visit for anyone looking to purchase authentic Maasai souvenirs.

Kazuri Beads, Nairobi: Kazuri Beads is a women's cooperative that produces beautiful and hand-painted ceramic beads, pottery, and ceramics. The cooperative employs disadvantaged women, and their shop in Karen, Nairobi, is a great place to buy unique and meaningful gifts.

City Market, Nairobi: Situated in the heart of Nairobi, City Market is a one-stop shop for traditional Kenyan crafts, jewelry, clothing, and local food products. It's a convenient place to explore Kenyan culture and shop for souvenirs

Biashara Street, Nairobi: Biashara Street in Nairobi's central business district is a bustling shopping hub, offering a wide range of goods from clothing and accessories to electronics and more. It's a great place to practice your bargaining skills.

Lamu Island, Lamu Archipelago: Lamu Island is known for its charming narrow streets lined with shops selling traditional Swahili and Lamu crafts. The island is particularly famous for its intricately carved wooden doors, which make unique and striking souvenirs.

Gikomba Market, Nairobi: Gikomba Market is one of Nairobi's largest second-hand clothing markets. Here, you can hunt for unique clothing, shoes, and accessories at budget-friendly prices. Be prepared to explore and negotiate for the best deals.

Sarit Centre, Nairobi: Sarit Centre is a modern shopping mall in Westlands, Nairobi. It features a variety of stores selling clothing, electronics, and accessories. It's a convenient option for those looking for brand-name products.

Masai Flea Market, Malindi: If you're exploring the coastal town of Malindi, don't miss the Masai Flea Market. This market offers a selection of Masai jewelry, clothing, and other African crafts, making it a great place to shop for coastal-inspired souvenirs.

Popular Souvenirs

Beaded Jewelry: Beaded jewelry is a signature souvenir of Kenya, especially from the Maasai and Samburu communities. Look for intricate beaded necklaces, bracelets, and earrings that showcase traditional designs and vibrant colors.

Wooden Carvings: Wooden carvings are another popular choice. These intricate pieces of art range from animal sculptures and masks to functional items like salad servers and utensils. Lamu Island is famous for its woodwork.

Kangas and Kitenges: Kangas and kitenges are brightly colored, printed fabrics that are often worn as wraps. They make fantastic souvenirs and come in a variety of patterns and designs.

Maasai Shukas: Maasai shukas, or blankets, are known for their distinctive red plaid patterns. They are versatile and make great gifts or home decor items.

Soapstone Carvings: Kisii soapstone carvings are meticulously handcrafted by artisans in the Kisii region. These carvings come in various shapes and sizes and often depict animals, people, and abstract designs.

Kenyan Coffee and Tea: Kenya is renowned for its coffee and tea. You can purchase high-quality Kenyan coffee beans or tea leaves to take home as a flavorful and aromatic reminder of your trip.

Bargaining Tips

Be Polite: Politeness goes a long way when bargaining. Start with a friendly greeting and a smile, and maintain a positive attitude throughout the negotiation.

Know Your Budget: Before you start bargaining, have a clear idea of your budget and the maximum price you're willing to pay. This will help you negotiate more effectively.

Start Low: Begin your negotiation with a lower price than you're willing to pay. This provides room for the seller to make a counteroffer, which can lead to a more favorable deal.

Be Willing to Walk Away: Don't be afraid to walk away if the seller isn't meeting your price expectations. In many cases, this will prompt the seller to offer a lower price to close the deal.

Don't Rush: Take your time during the bargaining process. Bargaining is a social activity in many Kenyan markets, and it's essential to build rapport with the seller.

Enjoy the Experience: Bargaining can be an enjoyable part of shopping in Kenya. Embrace the cultural exchange and the chance to interact with local artisans and vendors.

Shopping in Kenya is an opportunity to bring home unique and meaningful souvenirs while experiencing the local culture and customs. Whether you're exploring vibrant markets, discovering intricate beaded jewelry and wooden carvings, or bargaining with friendly vendors, the process of selecting and purchasing souvenirs is a memorable part of your journey through this captivating country.

CULTURAL FESTIVALS AND EVENTS

Kenya is a country rich in culture and traditions, and one of the best ways to experience this cultural tapestry is by attending its diverse festivals and events.

In this chapter, we'll delve into some of Kenya's most prominent cultural festivals and events, including the awe-inspiring Wildebeest Migration, the vibrant Lamu Cultural Festival, the unique Maralal Camel Derby, the music and food extravaganza of the Koroga Festival, and the serene Lamu Yoga Festival.

Wildebeest Migration

The Great Migration: The Great Migration is one of the most remarkable wildlife events on the planet. Each year, millions of wildebeest, zebra, and other herbivores migrate from the Serengeti in Tanzania to the Maasai Mara in Kenya in search of fresh grazing grounds. This natural spectacle is a true testament to the circle of life in the animal kingdom.

Timing the Migration: The migration typically occurs between July and September. It's crucial to plan your visit during this time to witness the wildebeest crossing the Mara River, braving crocodile-infested waters, and facing predators on the other side.

Spectacular Game Viewing; The migration offers unparalleled game-viewing opportunities, with predators like lions and cheetahs following the herds, and countless opportunities to witness the circle of life in the wild.

Where to Stay: Accommodations around the Maasai Mara, including luxury lodges, tented camps, and budget-friendly options, allow you to experience this wildlife spectacle in comfort.

Lamu Cultural Festival

A Celebration of Swahili Culture: The Lamu Cultural Festival is a vibrant celebration of Swahili culture and heritage on Lamu Island. This annual event provides an immersive experience of the traditions and practices of the Swahili people.

Dhow Races: Dhow races are a highlight of the festival, where traditional wooden sailing boats compete in friendly but fierce races along the Indian Ocean coast.

Traditional Dances and Music: Enjoy the mesmerizing rhythms and melodies of Swahili music and dance. Performances feature colorful costumes, and you can even join in the celebrations.

Local Cuisine: Savor the flavors of Swahili cuisine with dishes like pilau, biryani, and coconut fish curry. The festival is a culinary delight for food enthusiasts.

Art and Crafts: Explore the art and craft exhibitions, where local artisans showcase their intricate handiwork, including intricate wood carvings and beaded jewelry.

Maralal Camel Derby

A Unique Sporting Event: The Maralal Camel Derby is one of Kenya's most unique sporting events. Taking place in the town of Maralal in Samburu County, it features camel races that attract participants and spectators from around the world.

The Main Race: The highlight of the event is the grueling camel race, which involves riders from various nationalities competing in a challenging 10-kilometer circuit.

Cultural Performances: In addition to the camel races, the event features cultural performances and exhibitions, showcasing the traditions and practices of the Samburu people.

A Festive Atmosphere: The Maralal Camel Derby is more than just a race; it's a festive celebration that brings the community together and offers an extraordinary cultural experience.

Koroga Festival

A Fusion of Music and Food: The Koroga Festival is an exciting celebration of Kenyan music, culture, and cuisine. It combines live music performances with an array of delectable food offerings.

Top Musicians: The festival features live performances by some of Kenya's top musicians and bands, creating an electric atmosphere that resonates with fans of diverse music genres.

Food and Cuisine: Local chefs and food vendors serve a wide variety of Kenyan and international dishes, allowing attendees to explore the country's culinary diversity.

Art and Fashion: In addition to music and food, the festival often includes art exhibitions and fashion showcases, providing a platform for local artists and designers to shine.

Family-Friendly Fun: The Koroga Festival is a family-friendly event with activities for children, making it an inclusive experience for all.

Lamu Yoga Festival

A Serene and Mindful Gathering: The Lamu Yoga Festival is a unique event that brings together yoga practitioners, teachers, and enthusiasts in the serene setting of Lamu Island.

Yoga Workshops and Sessions: The festival features a wide range of yoga workshops, meditation sessions, and wellness classes. Whether you're a seasoned yogi or a beginner, you can find something to suit your level.

Holistic Well-Being: In addition to yoga, the festival emphasizes holistic well-being and offers activities like nature walks, wellness talks, and sound healing sessions.

Cultural Exploration: The festival also provides opportunities to immerse yourself in the Swahili culture of Lamu through traditional music and dance performances.

A Mindful Escape: The Lamu Yoga Festival offers a unique chance to escape the hustle and bustle of daily life, reconnect with your inner self, and find inner peace in a stunning coastal setting.

Kenya's cultural festivals and events provide a fascinating glimpse into the country's rich heritage and diverse traditions.

]Whether you're witnessing the awe-inspiring Great Migration, celebrating the vibrant Swahili culture at the Lamu Cultural Festival, participating in the unique Maralal Camel Derby, enjoying the fusion of music and cuisine at the Koroga Festival, or finding serenity and mindfulness at the Lamu Yoga Festival, these events offer experiences that will stay with you long after your journey through Kenya.

KENYA FOR FAMILIES

Kenya is not only a paradise for wildlife enthusiasts and adventure seekers but also an excellent destination for families. In this chapter, we'll explore family-friendly destinations, activities that cater to kids of all ages, and essential safety tips to ensure a memorable and worry-free family trip.

Family-Friendly Destinations

Nairobi: Kenya's capital city, Nairobi, offers a variety of family-friendly attractions. The Nairobi National Park, located on the city's outskirts, allows you to see wildlife without venturing far from the urban center. The David Sheldrick Wildlife Trust, known for its elephant orphanage, is a hit with kids.

The Giraffe Centre offers a chance to get up close and personal with these graceful creatures, and the Karen Blixen Museum offers insights into Kenya's colonial history.

Maasai Mara National Reserve: A family safari in the Maasai Mara is a remarkable experience. Children can marvel at the incredible wildlife, including lions, elephants, and zebras, in their natural habitat. Many lodges and safari camps in the reserve offer family-friendly accommodations and services, making it accessible for kids of all ages.

Diani Beach: Diani Beach, on Kenya's south coast, is noted for its white sandy shores and crystal-clear waters. It's a perfect spot for a family beach holiday, with various family-friendly resorts and aquatic activities like snorkeling, swimming, and beachcombing.

Lake Naivasha: Lake Naivasha is a calm freshwater lake in the Great Rift Valley, famed for its birdlife and hippos. You can take boat tours on the lake, visit the Elsamere Conservation Centre, and have picnics by the shore. It's a terrific site for nature-loving families.

Lamu Island: Lamu Island, part of the Lamu Archipelago, offers a unique cultural experience. Strolling through the narrow alleys of Lamu Town, learning Swahili culture, and enjoying the island's tranquil ambiance make it a family-friendly vacation.

Kid-Friendly Activities

Wildlife Safaris: Kenya's national parks and game reserves give a wonderful opportunity for children to view wild creatures in their natural habitat. Game drives, conducted by knowledgeable rangers, give a safe and entertaining experience.

Giraffe Feeding: The Giraffe Centre in Nairobi allows children to feed and interact with giraffes, making it a memorable experience. The conservation of these magnificent animals can be taught to the children.

Orphanage for Elephants: In the wild, baby rhinos and elephants that are orphaned are housed at the David Sheldrick Wildlife Trust. Children can learn about wildlife protection while seeing the animals being fed and playing at the orphanage.

Maasai Traditions: For kids, going to a Maasai village is an immersive and instructive experience. In addition to watching traditional dances and learning about the Maasai way of life, they can even attempt Maasai jumping.

Adventure-Based Tasks: Kenya provides exhilarating experiences for families with older kids and teens, such as horseback riding in the Great Rift Valley, rock climbing in Hell's Gate National Park, and white-water rafting on the Tana River.

Summertime Recreation: Kenya's coastline is ideal for beach getaways with the whole family. Children can have fun discovering tidal pools, swimming in the ocean, and making sandcastles. Paddleboarding and snorkeling are two other water sports that are offered.

Acreage Jogs: In Kenya's national parks and reserves, take your family on nature walks. Children can learn about animals, plants, and insects while on guided excursions and taking in the breathtaking scenery of nature.

Safety Advice

Hepatitis: Ensure that all family members have received the appropriate immunizations before departing for Kenya. In addition, think about packing bug repellant and taking malaria prophylactics.

Keep Your Water Up: It can get hot in Kenya, so make sure your family drinks enough of water while traveling. Always have water on hand, and promote frequent hydration, particularly during outdoor activities like safaris.

Sunscreen Use: Cover your family up with caps, sunglasses, and sunscreen to protect them from the intense African sun. It's quite important when going on outdoor adventures.

Safety of Insects: When it comes to locations where diseases spread by insects are a problem, use insect repellent and think about dressing in long sleeves, especially at night.

Safety of Wildlife: You must always heed the advice of your guides and rangers whether you are in national parks or on safari. Never feed or approach wild animals; instead, keep a safe distance away from them.

Safety of Water: Make sure you abide by the safety precautions when swimming and participating in water sports if your family enjoys these activities. Kids should always be supervised near water.

Sensitivity to Culture: Instruct your kids about regional traditions and practices to promote polite relationships with neighboring communities. For example, when visiting rural areas or cultural places, dress modestly.

Remain in Unity: Families must stay together in crowded or strange areas. Establish a meeting spot or always have a cell phone on you to stay in touch.

Travelers with children of all ages will find Kenya to be a wonderful vacation due to its varied and family-friendly options. A family vacation to Kenya promises amazing experiences, whether you're exploring national parks, engaging with wildlife, experiencing local culture, or just taking in the breathtaking natural beauty of the nation. Making wise decisions and adhering to safety precautions can ensure that your trip is both entertaining and enlightening.

ETHICAL AND CONSCIENTIOUS TRAVEL

In addition to allowing visitors to take in Kenya's natural beauty and cultural richness, sustainable and ethical tourism also helps local communities, the environment, and wildlife protection. We'll look at the strategies and actions that enable you to travel responsibly in Kenya in this chapter.

The Conservation of Wildlife

Conservation's Big Five: The "Big Five" of Kenyan wildlife—lions, elephants, buffalo, leopards, and rhinoceroses—are well-known. The preservation of these recognizable creatures is the focus of numerous projects and organizations. By going to the projects and making contributions, you may help them in their endeavors.

The Wildlife Trust of David Sheldrick: The goal of this trust is to save and rehabilitate orphaned rhinos and elephants. You may see how these animals are cared for and learn about the difficulties they face by visiting the trust's Nairobi nursery.

The Center for Giraffes: The endangered Rothschild's giraffe is the main focus of the Nairobi Giraffe Center's conservation efforts. Participating in giraffe feeding events and attending them helps to support the conservation efforts of these animals.

Rhino Conservation in Ol Pejeta Conservancy: The only two northern white rhinos on the planet can be found in Ol Pejeta Conservancy. You may support the conservancy's continuing work and learn about it by visiting them.

Community-Based Tourism

Maasai Cultural Experiences: The unique culture and customs of the Maasai people are well-known. By participating in community-based tourism programs, such as visits to Maasai villages, you may support local businesses while learning about their way of life.

Samburu and Turkana Communities: Traveling to the northern Kenyan settlements of Turkana and Samburu offers a chance to experience their customs and traditions while helping the local people.

Projects Using Maasai Beads: Buying Maasai crafts and beading from neighborhood cooperatives and community initiatives guarantees that the money raised will go directly toward helping Maasai women and their families.

Conservations in Maasai Mara: The Maasai Mara Reserve is surrounded by numerous community-owned and managed conservancies. In addition to offering a personal safari experience, lodging at these conservancies directly supports the local economy.

Eco-Friendly Accommodations

Luxury Eco-Lodges: Kenya has several opulent eco-lodges and tented camps that emphasize eco-friendliness and conscientious tourism. These accommodations encourage neighborhood communities, reduce trash, and use renewable energy.

Camps and Lodges in National Parks: Numerous resorts and campers found in national parks and conservancies emphasize environmentally conscious operations, guaranteeing that your encounter with the local animals complies with guidelines for responsible tourism.

Eco-Friendly Practices: Kenyan eco-friendly lodgings frequently employ solar energy, water conservation, and trash minimization techniques. They also take part in initiatives for wildlife protection and community development.

Reducing Your Environmental Impact

Sustainable Transportation: Select environmentally responsible means of transportation when visiting Kenya. Select domestic flights to lessen traffic on the roads, and think about participating in carbon offset programs to lessen the environmental impact of your trip.

Reduce Plastic Waste: Use reusable shopping bags and water bottles to lessen your dependency on single-use plastics. Take note of any local laws about plastic bags—some parts of Kenya have outlawed them.

Support Responsible Tour Operators: Choose tour companies and guides that encourage ethical wildlife viewing and lend support to neighborhood projects. Make sure they observe moral guidelines when observing wildlife.

Respect Wildlife: Observe your guides and rangers' instructions when on safaris and during wildlife encounters to make sure you keep a respectful distance from animals and don't interfere with their natural activities.

Cultural Sensitivity: Respect the customs and cultures of the communities you come across. Dress modestly, get permission before snapping pictures, and make ethical purchases of locally made products.

Volunteer and Support Conservation Efforts: Think about supporting regional conservation organizations or taking part in activities aimed at protecting animals. These programs are essential to preserving Kenya's distinctive wildlife and flora.

Education and Advocacy: Inform yourself and others about Kenya's need for responsible travel and conservation. Encourage environmentally and wildlife-friendly legislation and push for sustainable practices.

Kenya's unique culture and stunning scenery are priceless assets that should be appreciated through ethical and sustainable travel. You can make sure that your travels not only enhance your own experience but also positively impact the preservation of Kenya's amazing natural heritage and the well-being of its communities by getting involved in wildlife conservation efforts, supporting community-based tourism initiatives, selecting eco-friendly lodging, and minimizing your environmental impact.

Conclusion

Your trip to Kenya has been an immersive investigation of a nation that enthralls its breathtaking scenery, abundant animals, lively cultures, and gracious people. Kenya has left a lasting impression on your heart and memories, from the busy streets of Nairobi to the magnificent savannahs of the Maasai Mara, the tranquil shores of Diani Beach, and the amazing views of Mount Kenya.

When you think back on your journey, it's critical to acknowledge the profound influence your travels can have on the locations you visit. You've aided in the preservation of Kenya's natural wonders, bolstered local economies, and promoted the protection of endangered animals by adopting sustainable and ethical travel habits.

However, your trip to Kenya need not end here. Your life will continue to be inspired and enhanced by the experiences, people, and memories you've had. You may spread the word about your amazing journey across Kenya, inspiring others to visit this amazing nation and advancing ethical and sustainable travel.

Think about telling friends and family about your experiences on social media, on travel blogs, or during chats. Others may be inspired by your tales to set out on similar adventures, which will increase awareness of Kenya's natural beauty and the value of conserving its cultural legacy.

Your trip across Kenya is proof of the transforming, enlightening, and inspiring effects of travel. It serves as a reminder of the value of discovering our planet, appreciating its diversity, and cooperating to preserve its treasures for the next generations.

Therefore, allow the spirit of this voyage to continue guiding you, whether you're organizing your next journey or just thinking back on Kenya. Both to you and to the amazing nation that has shared its beauty and culture with you, your journey through Kenya is a gift that keeps on giving.

APPENDICES

Travel Resources

A successful and stress-free journey to Kenya requires access to reliable information, useful tools, and helpful contacts. In this chapter, we'll provide you with a range of resources to make your trip to Kenya more enjoyable, organized, and safe.

Useful Websites and Apps

Kenyatta International Airport (KIA) Website

Kenya Airports Authority operates KIA, Nairobi's primary international airport. Their website provides essential information about the airport, including services, facilities, and flight details.

KENYA WILDLIFE SERVICE (KWS)

KWS is responsible for Kenya's national parks, reserves, and wildlife conservation. Their website offers valuable information on entry fees, park rules, and updates on park conditions.

SAFARICOM MOBILE APP

Safaricom is Kenya's leading mobile network provider, and their mobile app helps you manage your phone services, mobile money, and more.

IOVERLANDER

For the adventurous traveler, iOverlander is a useful app for finding campsites, hostels, and other resources while on the road.

XE CURRENCY CONVERTER

XE is a reliable app for currency conversion, helping you understand exchange rates and convert your home currency to Kenyan Shillings.

KENYA TRAVEL GUIDE (BY TRIPOSO)

This Kenya Travel Guide app provides information on places to visit, offline maps, and useful travel tips.

Emergency Contacts

Police: 999 or 112

Ambulance: 999 or 112

Fire: 999 or 112

16.8 Medical Assistance

AMREF Flying Doctors: +254 20 699 2000

International SOS (Nairobi): +254 20 272 4400

Nairobi Hospital: +254 20 284 5000

EMBASSY CONTACTS

United States Embassy (Nairobi): +254 20 363 6000

UK High Commission (Nairobi): +254 20 287 3000

Australian High Commission (Nairobi): +254 20 4277 100

TOUR OPERATORS AND GUIDES

Absolute Holiday Safaris

Basecamp Explorer

Gamewatchers Safaris

Intrepid Travel

LOCAL GUIDES

Maasai Guides in Maasai Mara

Samburu Guides in Samburu National Reserve

SAFARI COMPANIES

SafariBookings

Go2Africa

TRAVELER'S ITINERARY

3 Days in Kenya

Day 1 - Nairobi:

Visit Nairobi National Park.

Explore the David Sheldrick Wildlife Trust.

Enjoy dinner in the Karen neighborhood.

Day 2 - Maasai Mara:

Take a morning flight to Maasai Mara.

Enjoy an afternoon safari.

Stay at a Maasai Mara camp or lodge.

Day 3 - Maasai Mara:

Enjoy an early morning safari.

Witness the Great Migration (seasonal).

Fly back to Nairobi in the afternoon.

5 Days in Kenya

Day 1 - Nairobi:

Follow the 3-day Nairobi itinerary.

Day 2 - Maasai Mara:

Follow the 3-day Maasai Mara itinerary.

Day 3 - Lake Naivasha:

Visit Lake Naivasha.

Take a boat ride and see hippos.

Stay at a lakeside lodge.

Day 4 - Hell's Gate National Park:

Explore Hell's Gate National Park.

Hike and see geothermal activity.

Return to Nairobi in the evening.

Day 5 - Nairobi:

Explore local markets.

Visit the Karen Blixen Museum.

Depart from Nairobi.

7 Days in Kenya

Day 1 - Nairobi:

Follow the 3-day Nairobi itinerary.

Day 2 - Maasai Mara:

Follow the 3-day Maasai Mara itinerary.

Day 3 - Lake Naivasha:

Follow the 5-day Lake Naivasha itinerary.

Day 4 - Hell's Gate National Park:

Follow the 5-day Hell's Gate itinerary.

Day 5 - Amboseli National Park:

Drive to Amboseli National Park.

Enjoy an afternoon safari.

Stay at an Amboseli lodge or camp.

Day 6 - Amboseli National Park:

Enjoy an early morning safari.

View Mount Kilimanjaro.

Return to Nairobi in the evening.

Day 7 - Nairobi:

Explore local museums.

Shop for souvenirs.

Depart from Nairobi.

Whether you have 3, 5, or 7 days to explore Kenya, the itineraries provide a balanced mix of wildlife encounters, cultural experiences, and beautiful landscapes. Remember to adapt the checklist to your preferences and travel dates.

With the right resources, emergency contacts, reputable tour operators, and well-planned itineraries, your journey through Kenya will be filled with adventure, cultural insights, and unforgettable experiences. Safe travels!

Travel checklist

Passport and Visa: Ensure your passport is valid for at least six months beyond your intended departure date from Kenya. Check and obtain the necessary visa.

Travel Insurance: Purchase comprehensive travel insurance that includes coverage for medical emergencies, trip cancellations, lost luggage, and any specific activities you plan to engage in, such as safaris or adventure sports.

Vaccinations: Visit your healthcare provider for necessary vaccinations and medications. Ensure you have proof of yellow fever vaccination if required.

Prescription Medications: If you take prescription medications, make sure you have an ample supply for the duration of your trip.

Visa and Health Documents: Make photocopies of important documents, such as your passport, visa, and vaccination records. Store them separately from the originals.

Travel Itinerary: Create a detailed itinerary with important contact information, accommodation details, and flight information.

Emergency Contacts: Compile a list of emergency contact numbers, including your country's embassy or consulate in Kenya.

Currency: Exchange some currency (Kenyan Shillings) before your trip or upon arrival at the airport.

Adapters and Chargers: Bring the appropriate travel adapters for your electronic devices, as Kenya uses Type G electrical outlets.

Local Currency: Familiarize yourself with the local currency, the Kenyan Shilling (KES), and research current exchange rates.

Language: Learn a few basic Swahili phrases to facilitate communication.

Miscellaneous:

Travel Guide: Bring a travel guidebook or use travel apps for reference.

Sunglasses: To protect your eyes from the strong African sun.

Reusable Water Bottle: Stay hydrated and reduce single-use plastic waste.

Travel Locks: Secure your luggage and valuables.

Entertainment: Books, magazines, or entertainment for the journey.

Travel Pillow and Blanket: For comfort during long flights or road trips.

Travel Adapters: Make sure you have the right adapters for Kenyan electrical outlets.

Small Backpack: For day trips and excursions.

Remember that the specific items you need may vary based on your travel plans and preferences, so adapt this checklist to your individual needs and travel style. Safe travels!

Useful Phrases

Hello - Jambo

Good morning - Habari za asubuhi

Good afternoon - Habari za mchana

Good evening - Habari za jioni

Good night - Usiku mwema

Common Phrases:

Yes - Ndiyo

No - Hapana

Please - Tafadhali

Thank you - Asante

You're welcome - Karibu

Excuse me / Sorry - Samahani

I don't understand - Sifahamu

How much does this cost? - Hii ni bei gani?

What is your name? - Jina lako nani?

My name is... - Jina langu ni...

Where is...? - ...iko wapi?

Help! - Saidia!

Directions:

Left - Kushoto

Right - Kulia

Straight ahead - Moja kwa moja

Where is the bathroom? - Choo iko wapi?

I'm lost – Nimepotea

Numbers:

1 - Moja

2 - Mbili

3 - Tatu

4 - Nne

5 - Tano

10 - Kumi

20 - Ishirini

100 - Mia

Eating and Drinking:

Water - Maji

Food - Chakula

I'm a vegetarian - Mimi ni mpishi wa mboga

The bill, please - Bili, tafadhali

I would like... - Ningependa...

Water, please - Maji, tafadhali

Cheers! - Kwa afya!

Time and Dates:

Today - Leo

Tomorrow - Kesho

Yesterday - Jana

What time is it? - Ni saa ngapi?

Days of the week:

Monday - Jumatatu

Tuesday - Jumanne

Wednesday - Jumatano

Thursday - Alhamisi

Friday - Ijumaa

Saturday - Jumamosi

Sunday - Jumapili

Emergencies:

Help! - Saidia!

I need a doctor - Nahitaji daktari

I'm lost - Nimepotea

Call the police - Piga polisi

Shopping:

How much does this cost? - Hii ni bei gani?

I'll take it - Nitachukua hii

These phrases should be helpful for everyday interactions during your trip to Kenya. Swahili is widely spoken, especially in urban areas, and using these phrases can enhance your travel experience and make it easier to connect with the friendly locals.

Printed in Great Britain
by Amazon